Garden ENCYCLOPEDIA

Rufus Bellamy

Published 2009 by
A & C Black Publishers Ltd.
36 Soho Square, London, W1D 3QY
www.acblack.com

ISBN HB 978-1-4081-0857-4
    PB 978-1-4081-1296-0

Series consultant: Gill Matthews

Text copyright © 2009 Rufus Bellamy

This book is produced using paper that is made from wood grown in managed, sustainable forests. It is natural, renewable and recyclable. The logging and manufacturing processes conform to the environmental regulations of the country of origin.

Produced for A & C Black by Calcium.
Printed and bound in China by C&C Offset Printing Co.

All the internet addresses given in this book were correct at the time of going to press. The author and publishers regret any inconvenience caused if addresses have changed or sites have ceased to exist, but can accept no responsibility for any such changes.

Acknowledgements
The publishers would like to thank the following for their kind permission to reproduce their photographs:
Cover: Istockphoto: Mammamaart; Shutterstock: Tischenko Irina. **Pages:** Dreamstime: Claudio Baldini 15t, Clearviewstock 8–9, Marika Eglite 9t, Noah Golan 14–15b, Irochka 1br, 16br, David Job 20b, Steve Mann 19, Megejaz 21r, Anette Linnea Rasmussen 13b, Jean Schweitzer 2, Kimberly Skeie 1bl, 16bl, Ljupco Smokovski 16c, Maxim Tupikov 11b, Olga Zinatova 8b; FLPA: Michael Durham/Minden Pictures 20t; Istockphoto: Catman73 4l, Danny Chung 1–24, Eric Isselee 7t, Hans Slegers 17br, Andrew Whittle 6bl, Alexei Zaycev 18t; Shutterstock: Abrakadabra 17bl, Shironina Lidiya Alexandrovna 5t, Argus 17bc, Elena Butinova 18b, Ziga Camernik 11t, Laurent Dambies 20–21, Sergiy Goruppa 1b, 16b, Jeff Gynane 14b, Hardtmuth 1t, 16t, Petr Jilek 10t, Els Jooren 4r, Wendy Kaveney Photography 17t, Kmitu 5b, Letty17 13t, Mashe 12t, Amy Myers 6t, PeapPop 15b, Kateryna Potrokhova 8t, Sally Scott 14t, Lori Skelton 3r, Szabo Photography 21t, Robert Taylor 6br, Andy Z 12–13b.

Contents

Backyard Safari

Come on a backyard safari to discover the world of wildlife in your garden, school ground, or local park.

Wildlife secrets: In this book you'll get to discover the secrets of amazing animals and plants that live just outside your window.

Seasons: The natural world changes as the **seasons** change, so there is always something new to see.

Blackbirds visit gardens to look for food.

Important places: Gardens and green spaces in towns and cities are very important. They provide animals with food and water, and a place to shelter and live.

Hedgehogs hunt in gardens for slugs and snails to eat.

Wildlife havens: Many animals are finding it more difficult to live in the countryside. This means that millions of gardens in Britain are now havens for a lot of wild animals such as hedgehogs and frogs.

Green gardening: It is important to make gardens as wildlife-friendly as possible. There is a lot you can do – from putting up a bird box, to making sure there are plants that provide food for insects, birds, and other animals.

The elephant hawk moth is just one of the amazing animals you might see in a garden.

On the Lawn

A lawn may not seem like a good place for wildlife, but look carefully and you'll be surprised at what you can find.

Grass: Like other green plants, grass makes its own food using energy from sunlight, water, and **carbon dioxide** from the air.

Take a look at the grass under your feet when you next play football.

Visitors: Lawns are places where you might catch a glimpse of the larger animals that sometimes visit gardens, such as foxes, hedgehogs, and rabbits. Birds also visit lawns to look for **minibeasts** and worms to eat.

Many birds eat worms they find in garden lawns.

Lawns: Many lawns are made up of three or four types of grass. Other plants such as moss, clover, and daisies also grow in lawns.

Worms: Under the lawn worms are busy eating the soil. This breaks it up and makes it better for plants to grow.

Minibeasts: Lots of minibeasts, such as ants, slugs, and snails, are found on lawns. Some minibeasts are not welcome. For example leatherjackets feed on grass roots and can damage lawns. Leatherjackets turn into daddy-long-legs.

Lunch on the lawn

Ants, slugs, and snails are just some of the small animals you can find in amongst the grass. Birds and other animals, such as hedgehogs, like lawns because the short grass makes it easier for them to find a meal.

In the Hedge

The overgrown bits around the edges of gardens, parks, and playgrounds are great for animals.

Hedgehogs: These prickly garden visitors feed on things such as slugs and worms. When the weather gets cold they make themselves a nest in a big pile of leaves and **hibernate**.

Nettles: Nettles can give you a nasty sting, but they are very good for insects. The caterpillars of many butterflies, including the small tortoiseshell and peacock, eat nettles.

Butterflies, such as this red admiral, lay eggs that hatch into hungry caterpillars.

Spiders trap food such as flies and other insects in their webs.

Brambles: Birds, insects, and other animals feed on the fruit that grows on plants such as brambles. This fruit contains **seeds** that animals often help to spread out. New plants grow from these seeds.

Spiders: Spiders spin webs using "spider silk" that they make in their bodies.

Ivy: The ivy plant is a great climber and can grow up a wall, fence, or tree. Climbing plants like this provide a place for animals to hide.

Spotlight on homes

Animals need places in which they can hide, shelter, and make their homes. That is why it is important to leave wild areas for animals in gardens, parks, and playgrounds.

Up a Tree

Trees, like the mighty oak, are home to many different animals – from the tiniest insects to large animals such as squirrels.

Fruit trees: Apples, pears, cherries, and other fruit trees don't just provide us with things to eat. Many animals, including birds and butterflies, eat fruit, too.

Large trees are a high-rise home for garden animals.

Evergreen: Trees such as yews and firs (the kind that are often used as Christmas trees) keep their leaves all year. These are called "evergreens". The trees that lose their leaves in the autumn are called **deciduous**.

Nests: Birds, such as crows, build their nests in the branches of trees. Other birds, like the bluetit, nest in holes. Putting up a bird box is a great way to give birds like this a home.

Old wood: A pile of old wood attracts many minibeasts including centipedes and beetles. It is also a place where animals such as frogs and newts can shelter.

Stag beetles like old or dead wood. They often live in tree stumps.

Fungus: Many types of fungus feed on dead and **decaying** wood.

Thirsty trees

Trees need water to live and grow. They take in water from the soil through their roots. The roots of a tree spread far out into the soil below it.

In the Flowerbed

The flowers and shrubs in a flowerbed are important for butterflies and many other insects.

Nectar: Flowers contain sweet **nectar**. Many insects visit flowers to collect nectar, which they use for food.

Ladybirds can eat thousands of aphids in just one year.

Roses: Garden flowers, such as roses, have been bred for their look and smell. Some gardeners also like to grow wild flowers, such as cornflowers and poppies.

Flowers and insects: Flowers make a powder called **pollen**. This is often rubbed off on insects such as bees, which then carry the pollen between flowers as they fly around. If this did not happen many plants could not make seeds.

Daffodils flower
in early spring.

Bulbs: Some flowers, such as daffodils, grow from an underground **bulb**. The plant uses food stored in the bulb to grow.

Ladybirds: Ladybirds are a gardener's friend because they eat aphids and other minibeasts that eat flowers. Many minibeasts can be found in a flowerbed, including centipedes, beetles, and flies.

Spotlight on snowdrops

The flowers of different garden plants appear at different times during the year. Snowdrops appear at the end of winter.

In the Vegetable Patch

Vegetable patches and **allotments** are where gardeners grow things to eat. They are also full of interesting things to discover.

Plant parts: We eat lots of different parts of plants. For example, we eat the roots of carrot plants, the leaves of lettuces, and the stems of celery.

The vegetable patch is a great place to find food — for both animals and people!

Potato: A potato is actually an underground food store for the potato plant. We dig them up and use them as food.

Compost: A garden compost heap is made up of old leaves, cut grass, and other garden waste. Worms and other minibeasts turn this waste into rich compost. This is put back into the soil to help plants to grow.

Pests: Many animals like to help themselves to food from a vegetable patch. Lettuces are a particular favourite of slugs and snails. Birds will eat newly planted seeds if they get the chance.

Peas: Look inside a pea pod and you will find seeds from which new plants grow.

A compost heap is a great way to recycle garden waste.

Each pea pod contains several peas.

Spotlight on slugs

Slugs are a pest to gardeners, but an important source of food for birds and other animals, such as hedgehogs. Slugs leave trails of slime behind them, so you can see where they have been.

In the Yard

Even an empty backyard with no grass and few plants can hold surprises for a wildlife explorer.

Night visitors: When it gets dark, a bright outdoor light, or lit window, will attract many insects, including midges and moths.
Bats eat these minibeasts.

Moths: Most moths fly at night and rest with their wings folded flat. Most butterflies rest with their wings above their backs – this is one way to tell moths and butterflies apart.

Ants: Ants are common garden visitors. They are small, but strong – they can carry over ten times their own body weight.

Ants like to hide away under stones and the cracks in walls.

It is important to feed birds in the winter when food is scarce.

Bird feeder: An easy way to attract birds into any yard is to put up a bird feeder, full of food such as seeds and nuts. Birds also need water, so put out a shallow dish of clean water, too.

Moths use the light of the moon to help them get about at night.

Dandelions: Dandelions grow in unexpected places – even in the gaps between paving stones.

Dangerous cats

Many garden birds and other animals are killed by cats, which often hunt them for food. Putting a bell around a cat's neck is a good way to warn away birds so they stay safe.

By the Pond

Many animals and plants need the water in a pond to live. It provides them with somewhere to find food and make a home.

Waterbeasts: Ponds are full of minibeasts. Some, such as pond snails, eat plants. Pond skaters run across the surface of the water to hunt other minibeasts.

Pond skaters are covered in hairs, which help to stop them slipping beneath the water's surface.

Danger: Remember, ponds can be dangerous, so be careful near them. Ponds can also be a problem for some animals, such as hedgehogs. It is important to provide a way for these animals to climb out.

Frogs and toads lay their eggs in ponds.

Frogs and toads: Frogs, newts, and toads live in and out of the water in ponds. They are **amphibians**. Frogs lay eggs called frogspawn. Tadpoles hatch from frogspawn, get bigger, change shape, and become adult frogs.

Algae: Algae grows in ponds and is eaten by many animals. In warm weather algae can grow very fast and turn pond water into something that looks like green slime.

This mayfly only has a short time to find a mate.

Spotlight on mayflies

Mayflies are one type of minibeast that lays its eggs in lakes, ponds, and rivers. The eggs hatch into nymphs. When full grown, mayfly nymphs leave the water. The adult mayfly then has less than a day to live.

In the Air

Gardens, parks, or yards are great places to see insects, birds, and other flying creatures.

Bats: Bats make high-pitched sounds that bounce off anything nearby. When bats pick up these echoes they know what is around them. This is how they catch insects in the dark.

Bats are usually seen in gardens at night-time.

Birds in a garden: Birds use gardens to search for food and water, and raise a family. House sparrows, starlings, blackbirds, and bluetits are among the common garden birds.

Robin: Birds like the robin sing to attract a mate and to mark out a territory. Male robins will fight fiercely to defend their territories.

Using binoculars will help you to spot birds such as this robin.

Migrating birds: Many birds are great travellers. Birds, such as the swallow, **migrate** thousands of miles from Britain to warmer countries at the end of summer. Other birds come to Britain from colder countries for the winter.

Spotting birds: If you want to get to know the birds that visit your garden, sit quietly in a hidden spot. You'll need a bird book to help you name the birds you see.

Spotlight on dragonflies

Dragonflies and damselflies are some of the most beautiful flying insects. They are also amazing hunters. They eat other minibeasts, such as midges.

Glossary

allotments areas of land that people use
to grow vegetables, flowers, and other plants

amphibians types of animals that spend part of
their time on land and part of their time in the water

bulb a part of a plant that stores food

carbon dioxide a gas that occurs naturally in the air

decaying when a plant or animal has died and is
breaking up into smaller and smaller pieces

deciduous trees or shrubs that lose their
leaves for part of the year

hibernate to go into a deep sleep to save energy and
survive the winter

migrate when animals move in search of food, a place
to breed, or to escape cold weather

minibeasts very small animals

nectar a sugar-rich liquid produced by plants
to attract insects

pollen a powdery substance produced by flowers

seasons the main divisions of the year – spring,
summer, autumn, and winter are the seasons in Britain

seeds tiny "baby" plants from which a new plant
will grow if conditions are right

Further Information

Websites

Find out how to encourage birds, animals, and insects into your garden at:

www.wildchicken.com/nature/garden/wild000_ wildlife_gardening_for_children.htm

Read a virtual garden wildlife diary at:

www.wildlifewatch.org.uk/wildlifediary

Books

All About Garden Wildlife by David Chandler. New Holland (2008).

In the Garden (Look What I Found!). Franklin Watts (2007).

Microscopic Life in the Garden by Brian Ward. Franklin Watts (2007).

RSPB Nature Handbook by Mike Unwin. A&C Black (2009).

Index